SIMPLIFYING CYBER

A BEGINNER'S POCKET GUIDE TO CYBERSECURITY

Yates Mondy

Mike Bowman

Simplifying Cyber
by Yates Mondy & Mike Bowman

Simplifying Cyber

Preface

Welcome to Simplifying Cyber, an introduction to cybersecurity for small businesses and organizations. If you are new to the field, or want to do something about cybersecurity but don't know exactly where to begin, then this book is for you.

Much of what is written about cybersecurity is *for* cyber professionals *by* cyber professionals, technically focused and often difficult to understand by anyone inexperienced or not living it every day. This leaves business owners and professionals in other fields unable to find the "so-what" and "take-aways" they can use to make their businesses more secure. That is not what you'll find here.

Instead we focus on easy-to-understand overviews, simplified guiding principles, and a cybersecurity program framework you can follow to save you time and resources in getting started. You'll get a quick introduction to the most critical cybersecurity fundamentals along with straight-to-the-point thoughts of how to move forward with creating *your* security plan, one specific to your needs. The security program framework is just that, a framework. It is not a checklist of specific actions because one size does not fit all. A family run construction company, a small medical practice, a financial services business, or a legal firm will all have different specific needs and concerns. However, following this one common framework will ensure that each is more knowledgeable and able to take the next steps to secure their businesses.

There is much more to learn about cybersecurity than just what is in these pages, but at the end of this book you will be well equipped with the knowledge to move forward with more confidence and understanding of cybersecurity and the Digital Age.

Simplifying Cyber

Contents

Introduction

Begin with the end in mind.

- Stephen Covey

The Internet has connected us in ways never before imagined, transforming our ability to have global impact. However, this same technology also amplifies others' ability to conspire, steal, manipulate, and attack with the same global reach, ease, and speed. We can no longer rely on time and distance to protect us; we must acknowledge and act as though any criminal in the world can impact our lives in an instant…because they can.

This pocket guide will give you the understanding and framework you need to start your journey to a more secure future, but remember it is only the first step. Up front we'll lay the groundwork by discussing the basic concepts of cyber risks and risk management, the Internet, cyberattacks, and cyber threat actors. These provide a solid foundation and are a necessary step to ensure the security program principles covered in the second half can be effectively applied to your specific needs and goals.

So as we begin, let's discuss how we got here and why we should all care about cybersecurity.

Why should we care about Cybersecurity?

The Internet was designed to be used by trusted people in a closed environment...we have been living with that short-sighted vision ever since.

- Unknown

Your information shapes your decisions, those decisions drive actions, and those actions determine your future. Information is the foundation of everything we do, good information leads to good decisions and better outcomes while bad information nearly always results in undesired consequences. In the Digital Age nearly all our information touches cyberspace somewhere, so cybersecurity is important to us all.

The Internet was born over a half-century ago as a way for trusted research organizations in different locations to collaborate and share knowledge. It was designed to enable high speed transfer of information, and since all users would be part of the same trusted groups, security was not a primary consideration. Then came the Internet and the World Wide Web.

Simplifying Cyber

Just as positive forces like research and commerce are enabled by the Internet, so too are negative. For years we have routinely heard of the major breaches at large corporations, however hackers are now increasingly going after "soft targets" like small businesses and individuals. They are doing this because smaller organizations don't have robust defenses; they are low risk - low effort targets offering a quick payoff where advanced hacking skills are often not necessary.

In just a few short minutes a hacker can craft and send a malicious email to your business...and a single mouse click can result in the theft of bank passwords or a ransomed network that leaves your business unable to function. It is a volume business for them, hackers know that one malicious email sent to 100 small businesses could have 50 or more successes...each of which could result in the emptying of bank accounts before anyone is the wiser. We aren't safer when we are smaller and less well known, we are easier targets.

We also cannot assume others can protect us. Laws often apply at the nation, state or local levels; but when we are attacked from different continents, law enforcement and other government organizations who normally protect us may not be able to act. Even if laws do apply and governments can provide some relief, it still may be very difficult to tell who perpetrated the act. Global cyberspace is occupied by everyone, but effectively governed and secured by no one. It is the new Wild West, and we are largely on our own to protect ourselves.

Most importantly, there is no such thing as impenetrable security. Cybersecurity is about reducing risk just as we do for fire or crime; no fire protection system or fire department can prevent all fires, no police force could stop all crimes, and no cybersecurity program can stop all cyberattacks. Unfortunately, cybersecurity risk management is less mature than other fields so many of us do not yet have the tools or knowledge we need to protect our businesses, networks, and information with confidence. The good news, however, is that with the information from *Simplifying Cyber* and a little preparation you can be well positioned to begin managing these risks yourself, or with a little professional help.

What is Cyber Risk Management?

There are risks and costs to action. But they are far less than the long-range risks of comfortable inaction.
- John F. Kennedy

We must take risks to move forward, and it is how we manage those risks that largely determines our successes or failures. A methodical risk management process is important everywhere, but especially in cybersecurity. It helps to ensure the security program you develop addresses your needs as effectively as possible, and that your resources are spent where they will provide the greatest value. A cybersecurity program is a necessary extension of normal risk management and good business practices, just like managing fire or crime risks.

Developing a standardized and repeatable approach for this risk evaluation will inform future processes, strategies, and decisions such as how to avoid, accept, mitigate, or transfer risk consistently in any situation. This standardized approach starts with understanding the components of risk and how they can be managed to reduce risk overall.

Components of risk

There are two fundamental components of risk, probability and severity. These two components are analyzed and then multiplied to give us a risk score or risk impact, an expression which helps us compare one risk to another as well as to management options. Risk impact could be either a specific number, such as a dollar value, or it could be a simple description such as low, medium, or high. Arriving at these values the same way every time is important to ensure accurate comparisons and informed decisions over time.

Risk strategy: Tolerance and mitigation

Tolerance for risk changes by individual and circumstance, so a consistent approach to determining risk impact also helps reduce unintentional biases in risk decisions. The first decision must confirm if a risk is acceptable or unacceptable based on the risk impact value. If the impact is small enough and the risk is tolerable, the decision is "risk accept" and the organization moves on. If the risk is unacceptable, then the decision must be to either "risk avoid" by taking a different path, "risk mitigate" through preventative or off-setting actions, or to "risk transfer" through a mechanism such as insurance.

Ideally, the probability and severity analysis gives a number such as a dollar figure to make things simple. For example, if you have a 90% chance of losing a $10,000 asset, the risk impact is $9,000. If that figure is acceptable, or if the cost to mitigate the risk exceeds the $9,000, then the decision is "risk accept." If that risk is not acceptable, then something must be done to reduce either the probability or severity until the impact is acceptable.

Unfortunately, specific numbers for cyber risks can be hard to determine. This is due to the lack of authoritative probabilities for cyberattacks and the many ways a business can be impacted, so best estimates must be used. Severity numbers are usually easier; businesses can understand and estimate impact for loss of tangible assets or processes such as payroll or billing. Running the numbers, even approximations or qualitative descriptions, ensures the best use of resources and is critical to making the best risk decisions.

Types of risk in cybersecurity

In cybersecurity there are three basic risk categories; Legal, Brand, and Technical. Each type presents a unique set of issues that must be considered, and are generally defined below:

Legal/regulatory risks are risks derived from non-compliance with standards identified and enforced by an appropriate authority (e.g. criminal charges for not following the law).

Brand/reputational risks are risks derived from adverse impacts enforced by societies or markets when we do not behave according to real or perceived societal standards. (e.g. lost sales after a breach of consumer data when all laws were followed).

Technical/existential risks are risks from direct malicious activity (e.g. ransomware halting operations or theft of trade secrets and loss of competitive advantage).

Legal and regulatory risks are the easiest to understand and quantify. Laws, rules, and contracts are recorded and nearly always available for reference, as are the penalties for non-compliance which could be financial or perhaps criminal. These risks are also the simplest to manage, follow the rules and you should be immune to the risks.

Brand and reputational risks are more difficult to assess and manage. Outcomes of large breaches against major corporations have shown that even without breaking the law, or being non-compliant with regulations, businesses can be impacted significantly by unhappy consumers and the court of public opinion. Mitigation is largely a matter of public relations, security posture related to your industry, and caring for affected customers.

The final, and most difficult to assess and manage, is technical or existential risk. Theft of intellectual property can erase competitive advantage, criminals can forge emails resulting in fraudulent payments or theft of banking passwords, and one employee can click on an email that allows ransomware to infect and spread across a network stopping a business in its tracks. Effectively managing these risks requires an informed, complete, and well executed program.

Now that we understand cyber risks in general, the next step is to become familiar with cyberspace so we can apply this understanding to our own operations in that environment.

What is the Internet?

We are all now connected by the Internet, like neurons in a giant brain.

- Stephen Hawking

At first glance the Internet may appear to be a place where many things happen in the blink of an eye, almost as if by magic. In actuality, it is a complex set of technologies and robust, globally standardized engineering that make it all possible. Ports, protocols, IP addresses, routing, and a myriad of other terms can make the Internet very difficult to fully comprehend, but there are models that help us simplify and understand it.

Every networked information system is a combination of five parts; hardware, software, data, network/telecommunications, and the user. Each of these components is a potential weak link in the security chain that can be attacked, so risks in each must be addressed if the entire system is to be defended. A basic understanding of these components and the larger Internet ecosystem is necessary to create an informed cyber risk management strategy.

We can illustrate how this model works with an example of a familiar Internet process, a user loading a webpage. The user turns on their laptop (hardware), opens a web browser (software), and requests a web page from their bookmark list. The computer then sends that request (data) through the business hardware and software ecosystem of routers, switches, firewalls, and gateways and out into the global network of Internet backbone routers, switches, fiber optic cables, et cetera (telecommunications network). Then it travels past the gateways, firewalls, routers, and switches at the other end to get to the server hosting the website. That server answers the request by sending the appropriate data back through that same process to the user's computer where the browser displays it in the proper format. Even that over-simplified description is complicated!

Instead, let's think of the Internet as a digital version of the Pony Express mail system. One rider hands letters to another and another and so on, until the letter reaches its destination. Each rider places his or her hands on the letter and, if they were so inclined, could open and read the letter before repackaging and sending on. The Internet works in a similar fashion. Understanding that information traverses many objects and entities across the Internet on its way to the destination, and that not all of them can be blindly trusted, underscores the need for sound cybersecurity practices.

Every component of the information system should be protected at some level, but how far should that go? An effective risk management program will identify and understand how your business uses each of those five information system components to inform strategy and increase security holistically. This approach is critical because failure in any of the components can compromise the entire chain.

For instance, if one invests in advanced technical defenses for software but allows attackers physical access to hardware, then they have likely wasted their time and money. Similarly, robust physical security at an office that has open firewalls, vulnerable software, and unencrypted data could be just as vulnerable...and worse, globally accessible. Finally, even the best technical defenses can be defeated by social engineering that targets the user. If someone posing as "the Help Desk" calls reporting a problem and needs the user's password to fix it, would they get the password?

Remember that this five-component model is a simplified version of how the Internet and information systems work. It provides a solid understanding of the basics and highlights how your security plan must account for all components, but it is far from complete. As we discuss cyberattacks in the next section, remember that each component can be targeted and used to compromise other components to get to the attacker's objective.

Understanding Cyberattacks

We will bankrupt ourselves in the vain search
for absolute security.
- Dwight D. Eisenhower

There are no silver bullets for cybersecurity, though many will try to convince you that their product is what you need. A better solution is to learn how cyberattacks work so you can make informed risk management decisions; if you want to stop a hacker, you have to think like one. Understanding how attacks are executed will help you recognize weaknesses in your organization and identify opportunities to prevent them.

In some industries, the chain of events that allows incidents to transpire is referred to as a Swiss cheese model. This methodology provides a visualization of how an incident occurs; when the vulnerabilities (holes) in multiple operational layers (slices) are aligned they create an exploitable path from one end to the other. If we can identify all the slices and holes, and ensure even one is out of alignment, the unfortunate event never takes place.

There are multiple similar methodologies that describe how cyberattacks occur, but perhaps the easiest to understand and most widely used is Lockheed Martin's Cyber Kill Chain®. The Cyber Kill Chain model describes how cyberattacks happen in seven distinct stages: KC1 – Reconnaissance, KC2 – Weaponization, KC3 – Delivery, KC4 – Exploit, KC5 – Installation, KC6 – Command & Control, and KC7 – Actions on Objectives. The argument is that, like the safety Swiss-cheese model, holes within all layers must be aligned and successfully exploited to execute an attack. This also means that each stage provides an opportunity to break the chain and prevent the final attack from happening.

For example, if an attacker Delivers a malicious email to a target (KC3), but the target's system has a security patch, then it cannot be Exploited (KC4) and the attack is stopped. If the system did not have the patch then the Exploit is successful and malicious software (malware) is Installed (KC5), but if network defenses prevent the attacker from achieving Command and Control (KC6) then the attack is stopped here. In both cases the attacker was prevented from progressing to their objective and achieving their desired final impact (KC7).

These same basic seven steps are executed for each attack regardless of the attacker's identity, target organization, or objective. The opportunity to block at each phase underlies the Defense-In-Depth concept, a technique that addresses risks not at one layer but at several. This ensures that multiple misses must occur before the attacker's endgame is accomplished. Defense-in-Depth also works with your risk management process to help you select which actions provide the highest Return on Investment, delivering the desired level of defense with the least cost.

Threat actors and profiles

In addition to the flow of a cyberattack, it is also helpful to understand different types of malicious cyber actors, what they do, why, and how. The general convention is that there are four basic types of malicious cyber actors; hacktivists, cyber criminals, advanced persistent threat actors (APT), and cyber terrorists. The primary difference between each is their motivation and available resources, which translate into capability and threat level, but more on that shortly.

> ***Hacktivists*** are politically motivated individuals or groups trying to leverage attacks to change public opinions and political outcomes. Their typical actions include website defacements, Internet postings, and other actions designed to grab attention to promote their message.

Cybercriminals are out for monetary gain. They may do anything to further that objective including direct theft or other indirect actions that can be recapitalized into money.

APT groups are usually defined as nation-state actors. They have access to the most advanced resources and typically have specific objectives to advance their national interests.

Cyber terrorists attempt to advance their radical agendas through any means available in cyberspace. This includes website defacement, criminal activities to raise funds, recruiting or inspiration of terror, or even destructive attacks against connected machines designed to instill fear.

Understanding these terms and differences is valuable because they are commonly used in the public space, however in the context of devising business defense strategy these distinctions are not exceptionally helpful. Instead, a capabilities-based model can more accurately inform what needs to be done to protect yourself from attack, no matter who is behind it.

Three Tiers of Actors

The following discussion describes three tiers of actors based on their capabilities. From these generalized descriptions, we can identify what types of cyber defenses are needed to protect us from that level of threat regardless of their motivation.

Tier Three actors present the least capable threats, often overt and unsophisticated. They use known tactics, techniques, and procedures (TTPs) that can be easily prevented with basic security controls. When properly defended Tier Three actors can be quickly mitigated and rendered completely ineffective, usually in an invisible and automated fashion that users never even see. However, if not countered, these high-volume threats can cause significant impacts.

Countering Tier Three is the foundation, it is where security must start for all organizations. Utilizing basic security controls and system hygiene, such as anti-virus and patching among others, will provide a reasonable level of security and may be enough for some businesses. The good news is that with the right knowledge, this level of security can be easy and relatively inexpensive to implement.

Tier Two actors are less common but more complex, they are able to act in a covert manner. Their tools and tactics are close to Tier Three but not an exact match for previously seen activity, something which increases the difficulty in countering them. Tier

Two actors can take known malware or TTPs and change them slightly so that Tier Three focused security can no longer defeat them before they infect a system or network.

The good news here is that Tier Two actors and their activities resemble known bad malware and TTPs. They can be found, and perhaps even prevented, through basic analytical-type detections and protections that many security products have built-in. These features are rarely enabled "out-of-the-box," but can be leveraged if you set them up correctly.

Not all businesses need Tier Two-level security, and even then probably only in higher risk areas. Engagement and risk management in this area requires more resourcing, so it should be based on organizational need with resources aligned to the decision maker's risk tolerance and strategy.

Tier One actors are truly exceptional, they are the most advanced individuals or organizations who can create their own malware and TTPs from scratch. Their tools are unknown so nobody knows to look for them, making them the hardest actors to find and mitigate. Tier One actors may even be using your legitimate business practices and systems to conduct their attacks with near-invisibility. These groups are extremely formidable, and effectively countering them is the pinnacle of cyber defense. They are ghosts in the mist.

The details vary between Tier One groups, but the commonality is that they all exist "in the noise" of everyday activities. They are invisible to all but the most thorough security practices and technologies, so effective mitigation requires significant discipline, diligence, vigilance, and investment. The goal for defenders should be to "see all" and ensure that anything "not known good" is found, assessed, and, if necessary, terminated to protect against these exceptionally capable foes.

The Security Program

The plan is nothing, planning is everything.

- Dwight D. Eisenhower

The Security Program is where all this knowledge comes together, delivering reduced risk and adding value to your business. Your understanding of risk, cyberspace, cyberattacks, and threat actors helps you develop specific goals for securing your information systems; the program is how you achieve those goals.

Large organizations have dedicated teams and budgets to develop and execute these programs, but that is a luxury most businesses simply cannot afford. While there is no substitute for a dedicated internal team, the good news is that the program principles can be adapted and applied to every organization. A good security program will address all of the topics we are about to discuss, although the steps should be scaled and tailored specifically to your needs and capabilities.

For some, cybersecurity may be a function you want to execute yourself with ongoing research, education, and experience along with some occasional outside help from professionals. Others may wish to outsource the cybersecurity function altogether, using the framework as a guide to ensure you are getting what you need instead of snake oil. Regardless, a sound understanding of this framework will ensure you are able to move forward with either path on your cybersecurity journey.

The focus of a security program is to achieve and maintain your information systems' Confidentiality, Integrity, and Availability; the cornerstones of information security.

> ***Confidentiality*** means only those users authorized to access information are able to do so. Your private information remains private.
>
> ***Integrity*** means your information cannot be changed or altered in any unauthorized way or by unauthorized users. Your information can be trusted.
>
> ***Availability*** means your information is accessible by users upon demand. It is always there when you need it.

The following sections are not a comprehensive cybersecurity checklist. They are a necessarily general guide for how to think about and create a living cybersecurity program that delivers Confidentiality, Integrity, and Availability aligned to your individual needs and objectives. It must be a living program because this is a dynamic field, no plan is perfect forever.

Policy

It all starts with policy. Policy is where responsibility is specified, authority given, goals stated, and high-level plan of action is created. Policy is especially critical in information and cybersecurity because the field is so diverse and can involve many different teams. Security, legal, compliance, and related teams often operate in silos, making true collaboration and teamwork difficult. As a result, the policy documentation becomes the cornerstone that ensures all efforts are unified and support a common goal, from the top to the bottom of the company. It is worth the time and effort to do well.

Leadership Roles & Responsibility

Even the greatest of plans and wisest of leaders will fail without effective implementation, and that requires responsibility and accountability enabled by authority. Additionally, risks change as business technologies and processes grow and evolve...not to mention threat actor capabilities. Your program leader must have vision and adaptability to ensure your program stays relevant through these transitions. A good security program leader ensures the program does not remain stagnant; they must always be planning because The Plan as written can become obsolete quickly. The importance of good leadership cannot be overstated.

Data Classification and Management

Data can be generated as a memo, a database entry, an email, or many other forms. It can be a proprietary technical diagram on a server, a sales invoice with sensitive account information, or a human resources database holding legally covered personal information. Although each data set is different, they each carry some form of sensitivity and thus risk to your business if compromised.

Data management starts with understanding and classifying your data into different categories, usually by subject matter and risk level, so it can be effectively managed. That data must be controlled properly through its entire life cycle; creation, sharing, modification, and destruction. Once your data classification and management process is framed and understood, the business leader can then begin the process of determining what steps should be taken to manage the applicable types of risk. That processes should begin with a legal, regulatory, and compliance review.

Legal, Regulatory, and Compliance Review

Once you know what data you have, you must find out what Legal, Regulatory, and Compliance requirements apply to your business. They can vary widely across industries, so consultation with legal and security professionals will help you clearly identify requirements and ensure they are implemented properly. Your implementation plan should start here because these regulations may generally, or even specifically, direct how you execute your program and secure your data.

Asset Identification, Classification, and Management

You must understand where your data lives before you can control and protect it. In the digital world, the information you need to protect resides on various assets such as servers, laptops, desktops, mobile devices, or in The Cloud. Tracking and controlling that information also requires tracking and controlling those assets, a process called asset management. Unfortunately asset lists change, sometimes often, so asset management must be a living process. Assets, like information, should be classified by risk according to their exposure, the sensitivity of their information, and the criticality of the processes they support. Only after this identification and classification is complete can they be managed by importance and risk level, including how and by whom they are accessed.

Identity and Access Management

Simply put, identity in cyberspace refers not to your person but to your digital self. It is how you "prove" that you are who you say you are. This proof is needed to control access to assets or data and is usually validated in one of three ways: something we know, like a password; something we have, like a card or token; or something we are, like a fingerprint. The strength of access control should be governed by an asset's risk, with increased diligence tied to increasing risk.

Defensive Strategy

Defensive strategy combines the situational awareness gathered from the earlier discussions and translates that into an actionable, risk-based plan. This plan should cover technology, architecture, staffing, and operations to provide the risk profile desired and resourced by business leadership. No matter the size of the business, the fundamental principles remain the same; Protect, Detect, Respond, Remediate, Recover, and Assess.

As you plan your strategy, all of these functions should be applied to your specific five component information system model, across every step of a cyberattack, and against every level of actor you are trying to counter. The resultant plan is how you achieve your goals and protect your business by ensuring the Confidentiality, Integrity, and Availability of your information systems.

Awareness and Training

After your defensive strategy is complete there are still a few other critical functions. One of these is security awareness and training because even advanced technical defenses can be defeated by one unsuspecting user divulging a password to a hacker or clicking on a malicious link in an otherwise normal looking email. An effective Security Awareness program can reduce your risk by turning every employee into a well-trained defender, potentially making more expensive technical solutions less necessary. A poor or non-existent program and unaware workforce might make your current expensive technical solution ineffective.

Validation

Internal validation is another important step because it is your first chance to discover a problem where you expect there to be none. This can be accomplished with your own staff, however there is usually more value and credibility in an external assessment. External validation may even be required by legal and regulatory frameworks, which might include audits or even Penetration Tests (ethical hacking) on a periodic basis. The important thing is to remember that without validation, we only think we know what the truth is.

Periodic Reviews

Periodic reviews are nothing more than the process undertaken at set intervals, whatever they may be, where the company assesses their security posture against new trends in security. The review then drives adjustments to mitigate any newly identified gaps. Even if no attacks have occurred, a new regulation may require you to change a technology or process, your old plan may no longer support your evolving business strategy and operations, or new resources may allow for additional investment you previously wanted but could not afford. In any case, it is worth it to ensure your plan is periodically revisited and updated to make sure it doesn't become obsolete.

Conclusion

We hope you enjoyed this short introduction to cybersecurity, and that you are taking away some good thoughts, questions, and themes that will help you in the future. A solid understanding of this pocket guide and its contents will help you develop specific goals for your business and take the next steps to securing your enterprise. That understanding will also ensure that you are able to effectively engage and have informed discussions with professionals who can help you accomplish those goals whenever you can't, or do not have the time, to do so yourself.

Remember that every cybersecurity plan must be as individual as the people, organization, and technology it supports...one size does not fit all! Furthermore, cybersecurity is not a static field. We must always be ready to learn and adapt to the world around us. That digital world changes every day as new technologies emerge, our business needs and processes change, and attackers learn and develop new ways to impact and steal what isn't theirs; we too must grow so we can stop them before they can. The Digital Age holds great promise to enable our businesses and improve our lives; access to global information and knowledge is a tremendous gift. However, that gift also comes with a great responsibility.

As you take your first steps with this new knowledge, above all else remember:

Your information is your future, secure it!

Author Biographies

Yates Mondy, Co-Founder & CEO of Arx | Cyber LLC

Yates's career has spanned many roles and responsibilities in the Information Domain over the last two decades. He began in active US military service supporting Navy, Joint, and Interagency task forces before launching a civilian career that has included contract project management for the research, development, test, evaluation (RDT&E) and operational needs of US government customers as well as a variety cybersecurity functions for one of the world's largest and most diversified multinational companies. Yates holds Masters' degrees in Cybersecurity Policy and Business Administration, and serves as a Commander in the US Navy Reserve.

Michael Bowman, Co-Founder & CTO of Arx | Cyber LLC

Mike started his career in application architecture for a small Industrial Systems firm supporting large corporate and government customers. Focusing early on asset tracking systems utilizing RFID and other scanning technologies, he gained extensive design and customer engagement experience. Looking to stay on the leading edge of technology, Mike made the jump to the Information Security Operations and Response organization in one of the world's largest diversified conglomerates. While there he held several strategic positions including Lead Coordinator for global information security incidents and Enterprise Security Architect, working large scale, complex, and strategic information security initiatives.

33352440R00028

Printed in Great Britain
by Amazon